IMAGES
of America

SAN BERNARDINO COUNTY
SHERIFF'S DEPARTMENT

IMAGES
of America

SAN BERNARDINO COUNTY
SHERIFF'S DEPARTMENT

M. David DeSoucy

ARCADIA
PUBLISHING

Published by Arcadia Publishing
Charleston SC, Chicago IL, Portsmouth NH, San Francisco CA

Printed in the United States of America

Library of Congress Catalog Card Number: 2006924917

For all general information contact Arcadia Publishing at:
Telephone 843-853-2070
Fax 843-853-0044
E-mail sales@arcadiapublishing.com
For customer service and orders:
Toll-Free 1-888-313-2665

Visit us on the Internet at www.arcadiapublishing.com

This book is dedicated to all the men and women of the San Bernardino Sheriff's Department, be they regulars, reserves, volunteers, or general employees, who have faithfully lived up to their oath. And especially to those sheriff's department personnel who died in the line of duty protecting and serving the citizenry of San Bernardino County.

Deputy Billy Heckle	EOW–January 1, 1960
Lt. Al Stewart	EOW–March 9, 1973
Deputy Frank Pribble	EOW–July 6, 1975
Deputy Clifford Sanchez	EOW–April 5, 1985
Deputy Donald DeMuelle	EOW–July 31, 1986
Deputy Keith Farley	EOW–April 12, 1987
Deputy Russell Roberts	EOW–September 17, 1995
Volunteer Scott Johnson	EOW–July 17, 2004
Volunteer Phil Calvert	EOW–July 17, 2004
Deputy Ronald Ives	EOW–September 1, 2004
Deputy Greg Gariepy	EOW–June 22, 2005
Deputy Danny Lobo Jr.	EOW–October 11, 2005

CONTENTS

Acknowledgments		6
Foreword		7
Introduction		8
1.	Wild and Western, 1853–1918	9
2.	The Shay Dynasty, 1918–1947	33
3.	The Transitional Years, 1947–1955	63
4.	The Frank Bland Era, 1955–1983	87
5.	"Dedicated To Your Safety," 1983–2000	105
6.	Millennium and Beyond, 2000–2006	121
Bibliography		127

ACKNOWLEDGMENTS

Many people assisted me in putting this volume together, and I would particularly like to gratefully acknowledge the following persons and organizations for their contributions to this volume. Without their mutual interest in history, contributions, and support of this project, the book would have been much more difficult to produce.

Thanks to San Bernardino County sheriff Gary Penrod for endorsing this volume and providing the foreword; Lt. Mike Stansell, Steven Jaronski, and Clark Morrow of the Public Affairs Division for all their assistance and photographs; Sgt. Patrick Dailey, retired Sgt. Richard "Dick" Bise, retired Inspector Paul Wilson, and former deputy and retired fire captain Duane Mellinger, who all provided much information and numerous photographs from their personal collections; Steven Shaw and members of the San Bernardino Pioneer and Historical Society for all their assistance and photographs; staff and volunteer docents of the California Room at San Bernardino's Feldheym Public Library for their assistance over the last several years; and my beloved wife, Angelika, who tolerated countless hours at our computer assisting me in meeting the specifications of the publisher.

FOREWORD

Way back in 1853, when Robert Clift took an oath of office as the first sheriff in San Bernardino County, the arrival of professional law enforcement was seen as an integral part of the advance of civilization in the Old West.

As crossroads and supply depots grew into towns, and as people followed explorers and fortune-seekers into remote areas, the need for a common code of behavior arose. More folks meant there had to be laws for all to obey, and the wild frontier needed to be transformed into peaceful communities. And of course, one of the very first needs in these communities was the need for law enforcement. A small town of men, women, and children presented a vulnerable target for those who fed on the goods of others.

The lawman was more indispensable than the mayor, the councilman, the teacher, or the doctor. Without him, there would have been no town in the first place. The little cities of the West revolved around their sheriffs and marshals and drew their very existence from them. As time went by, some of the sheriffs and marshals became police chiefs, and all of them—chiefs, marshals, and sheriffs—surrounded themselves with hired hands who helped to enforce the law in constantly growing jurisdictions.

This is the historical pattern that was followed in San Bernardino County. Watering places for horses became towns, towns became cities, the volunteer lawman became the sheriff, and the sheriff took on deputies, who multiplied to the point where currently they number almost 3,000 highly trained individuals. Some of these past sheriffs were in office for less than a year, and some of them (such as the towering, legendary figure of Frank Bland) reshaped the office through the length of their tenures and the power of their personalities. But all of them understood that the society being built in the western United States depended in every way on the strength and integrity of its law enforcement agencies. Nowadays, as a famous poet says, "It is difficult for those who live near a police station to believe in the triumph of violence." But back then, when "police stations" were few and far between, it was very easy to see that there could be no weddings or theatre shows or any other peaceful activities without lawmen of character standing guard in the heart of the city.

I am extremely proud to be a part of that history and a member of an organization that helped bring civilization to our part of the world. And I congratulate and thank Dave DeSoucy for telling us all so much about that history and this wonderful organization.

—Gary S. Penrod
Sheriff, San Bernardino County

INTRODUCTION

From an austere beginning in 1853 as a fledgling cow county sheriff's office, and with its continued development into a modern law enforcement agency of the 21st century, the San Bernardino County Sheriff's Department provides for a colorful, interesting, and intriguing history. This book was several years in the making, as it grew from an idea, to a concept, and final completion. It does not pretend to be the most comprehensive or concise compilation of that history but rather is offered up as a historical, pictorial overview. Some future author or historian will hopefully produce that volume. Many law enforcement agencies have comprehensive historical archives, museums, researchers, and societies. Unfortunately, over the years, there have been sheriffs and others who absconded or discarded many of the artifacts, documents, photographs, and records, thus much of the department's history has been lost forever. Likewise there have been few books or films done on the organization and its personalities. Most of its history is unknown to even the majority of the department members much less the public they serve. However, some department personnel, both active and retired, have assumed the roles of official and unofficial historians in their efforts to maintain that history. This historical volume honors those who came before and hopefully will contribute to further instilling a sense of cohesion, esprit, and service among its members and was produced in a humble effort to provide the reader with a glimpse of that history.

—M. David DeSoucy
Deputy Sheriff, San Bernardino Sheriff's Department, Retired

One

WILD AND WESTERN
1853–1918

The sheriff and his deputies from the mid-19th through the early 20th centuries wore most of the badges pictured. With the community being so small, most people already knew who the sheriff was, thus the early sheriffs may not have used a badge. With or without the badge, the first several decades in San Bernardino County certainly represented the phrase "the Wild West." (Courtesy of San Bernardino County Sheriff's Department.)

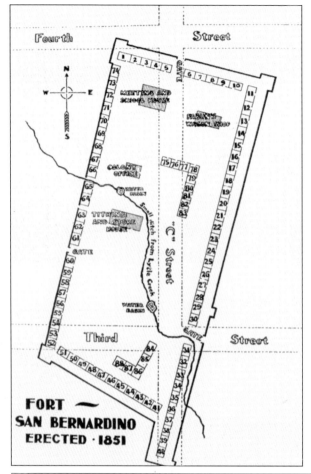

The Mormons moved into San Bernardino Valley in 1851 and established their new colony by constructing Fort San Bernardino for protection against the threat of marauding Indians and to maintain cohesion within the colony. Although Fort San Bernardino was in a portion of the sprawling Los Angeles County, the sheriff was in distant Los Angeles near the Pacific Coast, so the Mormons in their custom of justice handled law and order. (Courtesy of Richard Bise.)

Fort San Bernardino.
From the North East.
Oct. 1852.

The Mormon Council House, *c.* 1852, would serve as a church, post office, and school. With the establishment of San Bernardino County in 1853, the council house would be additionally used as the county courthouse. The first elected sheriff, Robert Clift, would also use it as a jail. (Courtesy of San Bernardino County Safety Employees Benefit Association.)

In 1856, Sheriff Clift attempted to evict Jerome Benson and associates from what became known as Fort Benson. After a land dispute was ruled in another's favor, Jerome Benson fortified the location and refused to leave. Sheriff Clift and his posse approached the fort when a cannon, loaded with stones, was fired at them. This caused the posse to pause, consider their options, and depart without further incident. The land dispute was eventually ruled in Benson's favor. In 1857, Sheriff Clift answered the Mormon recall to Utah, and Joseph Bridger was appointed the new sheriff and served until 1859. That same year, former sheriff Clift was murdered by Native Americans in Nevada. He was working as a sub-agent for the California and Salt Lake Mail Line, a forerunner of the Pony Express. (Courtesy of Richard Bise.)

Capt. Andrew Lytle served as a leader in the Mormon Battalion and was elected in 1856 as the first captain in command of the San Bernardino Rangers. The rangers would also be known as the San Bernardino Mountain Rangers and San Bernardino Mounted Rifles. The organization was a state-authorized and minimally funded militia unit, with its primary role being to assist the sheriff in maintaining law and order in the county. The rangers assisted several sheriffs in keeping the peace. Few documents have survived about their activities, but they did participate in mounted-posse manhunts and were deployed as a show of force during some of the turbulent times of the late 1850s and early 1860s. It is unknown why the organization was disbanded in 1862, when secessionist sentiments were at a peak in California. (Courtesy of Feldheym Library.)

Although marked otherwise, this jail cell, manufactured in 1860 from materials purchased in San Pedro, south of Los Angeles, was not the first. Constructed of a hand-riveted boilerplate, the cell was placed inside a jail constructed of stone. This remained satisfactory until the heavy rains of 1862 eroded the jail's integrity and was left exposed for several years. Much to the discomfort of the inmates, it functioned much like an oven in the summer and cold storage in the winter. (Courtesy of author.)

Sheriff Anson Van Leuven was the third sheriff to serve the county in the calendar year of 1860 and continued until 1862. Such were the growing pains of the fledgling county that Van Leuven was the sixth sheriff to serve between 1853 and 1862, with four more sheriffs serving in the two-year period between 1862 and 1863. He served during the turbulent times as the Civil War began and secessionist sentiment ran high. The gold strikes in the San Bernardino Mountains at Bear and Holcomb Valleys also caused him much concern as ruffians and shootings plagued the boomtown there. In 1861, Van Leuven led a posse of 17 men into the high desert seeking to apprehend two fugitives who had been making threats. While en route to the outlaws' location, an argument broke out amongst the posse members and boiled over into a gunfight. Four posse members were injured, two wounded quite seriously, and they had to return to San Bernardino to tend to the wounded. Van Leuven would go on to serve as a U.S. marshal. (Courtesy of Richard Bise.)

Sheriff Valentine "Rube" Herring was elected and assumed office in 1859. That same year, the Ainsworth-Gentry affair developed as a feud between the only two doctors in the county. One was a unionist and the other a secessionist. They insulted and assaulted each other with buggy whips and firearms. Both gathered local supporters, with Gentry also summoning Texas gunmen, then staying in the strongly secessionist town of El Monte. A gun battle ensued and four were wounded. Sheriff Herring rallied a "citizens' posse," and the gunmen retreated to El Monte. Sheriff "Rube" Herring served until 1860. Sheriff Charles W. Piercy was elected in the fall of 1859 and served until October 12, 1860, when he resigned to run for, and was elected to, the state assembly. He became involved in California's last political duel. He felt he had been insulted by State Assemblyman Don Showalter, so "Piercy issued the challenge." The duel took place on May 25, 1861, near San Rafael. Rifles were the weapons of choice, and the first rounds proved ineffective. Showalter "demanded another trial," which resulted in Piercy's death when he was fatally shot in the mouth. (Courtesy of Richard Bise.)

Due to the proliferation of saloons and related unsavory activities, the intersection at Third and D Streets in San Bernardino had the dubious title of "Whisky Point." The area was noted for attracting bad men and outlaws. Like many towns in the Old West, the area was also known for drunken rowdiness along with fistfights and gunfights. Sheriff Eli M. Smith won the fall election in 1861. His first order of business was forming a posse and pursuing the horse thieves that had been plaguing the county for several months. He and his posse "penetrated into the very camp of the outlaws, and carried off their booty." His posse captured three of the outlaws and recovered 40 horses. One local newspaper reporter stated, "Mr. Smith don't know any such word as fail." As a result of his tenacity, 18 men were sent to prison after being tried and convicted of horse thievery. (Courtesy of Richard Bise.)

Sheriff Benjamin F. Matthews was elected in 1863 and served for a year. He was a Mormon who contributed to the founding of the community but did not answer the 1857 recall to Salt Lake City. (Courtesy of Feldheym Library.)

George T. Fulgham served as sheriff from 1863 to 1869. In 1865, outlaw James Henry and his gang were known for everything from rustling to robbery and murder. In September of that year, he and his associates were camped out near San Bernardino and sent John Rogers to town to obtain provisions. While there, Rogers became "liquored up" and started boasting about his outlaw connections. The locals took note and Rogers found himself in the company of the sheriff and posse. At sunrise on September 14, the posse approached cautiously when Henry was awakened. He roused himself to fire three shots, striking one posse member in the foot. Henry died in a hail of shot and ball, having sustained 57 wounds. His corpse was taken back to town and displayed and photographed in Old West fashion. (Courtesy of Richard Bise.)

Some historians believe that Wyatt Earp's first law-enforcement experience occurred in San Bernardino County when he was 18 years old. There is evidence that in 1866 he participated as a member of a mounted group (posse) of citizens who were dispatched to reinforce Camp Cady in the high desert. Sheriff Fulgham led the posse, but the results were anticlimactic as there was no significant action involved. This photograph shows Wyatt Earp c. 1869. (Courtesy of *True West*.)

Construction on the San Bernardino County Courthouse began in 1873, and the halls of justice opened in 1874, with the sheriff's office being located inside and the jail in the basement. Some documents refer to the jail as the "courthouse prison." This arrangement was quite common in the 19th century and allowed for the sheriff and his deputies to securely move inmates to and from their courtroom appearances. (Courtesy of Patrick Dailey.)

Undersheriff John Mayfield, pictured here c. 1874, served under Sheriff A. J. Curry between 1873 and 1877. (Courtesy of San Bernardino County Safety Employees Benefit Association.)

Sheriff John C. King served San Bernardino County from 1879 to 1882. He followed Sheriffs William Davies (1877–1879), A. J. Curry (1873–1877), and Newton Noble (1869–1873) in serving the people of the county. King also served as a deputy for Sheriff James P. Booth from 1892 to 1894. (Courtesy of Richard Bise.)

San Bernardino was a sleepy, dusty town in the 1880s. (Courtesy of Richard Bise.)

Sheriff J. B. Burkhart is pictured officiating at the county's last execution by hanging. He arrived at this occasion as a result of the 1883 murder of a young girl named Maggie O'Brien, involved in a love triangle with the suspects, Mr. and Mrs. William B. McDowell. About a month after the ghastly deed, Mrs. McDowell came forward and confessed to the atrocious crime (although it is not known what happened to her). As the citizenry heard of the murder and as the sordid details became known during the trial, there was much talk of a lynching. The trial resulted in the murder conviction of William McDowell and an execution date was set for July 10, 1883. During the appeal process, William McDowell escaped from the jail and "a most exciting chase followed; he was recaptured, his sentence sustained, and carried out," according to one report. His end came on March 28, 1884. The gallows used for the execution became known as the "traveling gallows." They were constructed in San Bernardino, and for several years, the gallows were disassembled, shipped, and reassembled for use in Los Angeles, Santa Barbara, and Fresno Counties. In 1891, state legislation amended the practice of capital punishment to be conducted from then on in state prisons. (Courtesy of San Bernardino County Sheriff's Department.)

Sheriff J. B. Burkhart, who served the county from 1882 to 1884, is depicted here. (Courtesy of Richard Bise.)

After the Tombstone, Arizona Territory, gunfight and subsequent assassination attempt on his life, Virgil Earp moved to Colton to be near other family members. He became involved in local Republican politics and at one point considered running for sheriff. In 1886, he established the Earp Detective Agency and was elected as the constable for Colton Township the same year. It was common practice for constables to hold commissions as special deputy sheriffs both then and well into the 20th century. It is believed by some historians that this was the case with Virgil Earp. In 1887, he was elected as the first city marshal of Colton and reelected the following year. There is documentation indicating he ran his detective agency and served in both capacities as the city marshal and constable simultaneously. He also performed law-enforcement duties well beyond his primary jurisdictional boundaries during this time. These facts have led historians to believe he was also a special deputy sheriff. (Courtesy of *True West*.)

A sheriff's posse is pictured in the San Bernardino Mountains, c. 1890. The object of its quest is unknown, but due to the lack of displayed firearms, it is unlikely that they were on a deadly manhunt. (Courtesy of Feldheym Library.)

Sheriff Edwin Chidsey Seymour served San Bernardino County from 1888 to 1892. In 1883, he moved to San Bernardino and was a deputy sheriff under Sheriff Nelson G. Gill, who served from 1884 to 1885. In the fall of 1888, Seymour was elected sheriff. He was a member of the Grand Army of the Republic and several other civic and social organizations. (Courtesy of Richard Bise.)

Local "San Berdoo" peace officers are pictured around 1894 with San Bernardino city marshal and future sheriff, John C. Ralphs, seated in the doorway along with a deputy standing nearby—both in their brass-buttoned coats with badges. Others in the photograph are possibly constables or sheriff's deputies. (Courtesy of Steven Shaw.)

Voted for construction in 1892, the San Bernardino County Courthouse opened in 1898. The financial controversy over the structure, in addition to other issues, resulted in the breakaway and formation of Riverside County in 1893. (Courtesy of Patrick Dailey.)

The Daggett Jail, constructed of stacked two-by-four board, is pictured here c. 1895. It was used by the local constable and deputy sheriffs and is located on private property in Daggett. (Courtesy of author.)

Sheriff John C. Ralphs was the longest serving sheriff of San Bernardino County's formative years. Ralphs was elected in 1902 and served until 1915. Preferring the horse to the new automobile, he is considered to be the last horse-and-buggy sheriff. He would lead several of the last mounted-posse manhunts of the American Southwest. Two noteworthy manhunts were in 1906 when he and Undersheriff Samuel W. McNabb ventured out into the Mojave Desert and arrested "Death Valley Scotty" for instigating the Battle of Wingate Pass and in 1909 when he dispatched and led three posses during the hunt for "Willie Boy." (Courtesy of *True West*.)

In 1904, the county board of supervisors purchased several of these jail cells. Manufactured by the Barnum Iron Works Company, they were very heavy, yet portable, and used at various locations in San Bernardino County well into the 1960s. The last of these was installed in 1948 in the Argus Sheriff's Station near Trona. The cells are pictured here in front of the Mojave River Valley Museum in Barstow. (Courtesy of author.)

Dedicated in 1904, the county jail opened in 1906. It was a two-story sandstone building located on Court Street across from the first courthouse. It had offices along with matron, female, and general-population quarters. The San Bernardino County Board of Supervisors even authorized an expenditure of funds to install a telephone. Juveniles were also held in custody by the sheriff until the establishment of the probation department in 1909. (Courtesy of San Bernardino County Sheriff's Department.)

This is the sheriff's booking photograph of Willy Boy in 1905. He had been arrested for a disturbance at a baseball game in Victorville. In 1909, Willie Boy would become a fugitive in what has been called the "last great manhunt of the southwest" after having murdered the father of his captive bride. The story was told in Harry Lawton's book, *Willie Boy: A Desert Manhunt*, which was made into the 1969 film, *Tell Them Willie Boy is Here*, starring Robert Redford with Robert Blake as Willie Boy. (Courtesy of Dr. Larry Burgess.)

Pictured is the San Bernardino Police Department in 1906. Former deputy sheriff and future sheriff Walter Shay is in the front row, second from left. He served as the city's last marshal and first chief of police. (Courtesy of Feldheym Library.)

In 1907, Victorville constable Ed Dolch was responsible for the construction of this concrete jail. It was used until around 1948 by constables, highway patrolmen, and deputy sheriffs alike. The jail is now a city historical point of interest. (Courtesy of Arthur Banks.)

Newspaper reporter Randolph W. Madison, who accompanied the posses during the manhunt for Willie Boy, photographed Victorville deputy George Hewins in 1909 at Rock Corral near Ruby Mountain. He was the leader of the Victorville posse and had previously served as a town marshal in Nebraska. (Courtesy of Harry Lawton.)

Rather than being taken alive, Willie Boy committed suicide with his rifle at Ruby Mountain. Both San Bernardino and Riverside County posses are pictured posing with Willie Boy's corpse. (Courtesy of Patrick Dailey.)

Arrest for Double Murder

San Bernardino, Cal., Oct. 5, 1909

Willie Boy

A Chimehuevis Indian. 26 years old, about 5 feet, 10 inches in height; slim built, walks and stands erect; yellowish complexion, sunken cheeks; high cheek bones; talks good English with a drawl; has a scar under chin where he has been shot and some teeth gone. For years lived about Victorville, with a halfbreed American woman with two children, a girl of 10 and a boy of 2 years. She left him because he had beaten her, and returned to Victorville. His people living among the Kingston mountains, along the Nevada state line. He killed Mike Boniface, at Banning on the night of Sunday, September 26, and Ioleta Boniface, at The Pipes, in San Bernardino county, September 30.

An Indian filling the description of Willie Boy was seen cooking a rabbit between Goffs Station and Manvel on Sunday evening, October 3rd. When he saw the approaching parties he ran away. This might have been Willie Boy as his mother was at Vanderbilt a short time ago.
J. C. RALPHS, Sheriff.

Found dead Oct. 15-09.

This is Willie Boy's annotated wanted poster after his capture. There is evidence that suggests Willie Boy did not murder his captive bride but rather Riverside County posse members mistakenly identified her for Willie Boy and shot her at long range with a rifle. (Courtesy of Richard Bise.)

As the Old West passed on, Sheriff John C. Ralphs, pictured here around 1911, served out his term in 1915. (Courtesy of Richard Bise.)

Sheriff J. L. McMinn, seated at right, served only one term, from 1915 to 1918, and represents the end of the Wild West era of county law enforcement. He preferred the automobile to the horse and was involved in establishing county traffic enforcement. The county traffic officers, who were also commissioned deputy sheriffs, were formed in 1915. They rode motorcycles throughout the county, enforcing the county vehicle code. Sheriff McMinn was also involved in the establishment of the county road camps that same year. (Courtesy of San Bernardino County Sheriff's Department.)

This profile shot is another photograph of Sheriff J. L. McMinn. (Courtesy of California State Sheriff's Association.)

Two

THE SHAY DYNASTY
1918–1947

The sheriff and his deputies wore the badges pictured from the early 20th century into the 1960s. During the Roaring Twenties, the Depression of the 1930s, and war years, the Shay's kept the peace and maintained law and order utilizing new technologies along with the horse. (Courtesy of San Bernardino County Sheriff's Department.)

SHERIFF
WALTER A SHAY 1918-1931

Sheriff Walter A. Shay was quite the lawman. He began his career in 1899, serving four years as a deputy for Sheriff Charles Rouse from 1898 to 1902. In 1903, he was elected as the San Bernardino city marshal, serving in that capacity for two years before the mayor appointed him as the first San Bernardino chief of police in 1905. He also did stints with two railroads as a "cinder dick" in between two more terms as chief of police. He went on to become the chief special investigator for the district attorney before being elected sheriff in 1918. He served as sheriff until 1931 when he died from cancer while still in office. (Courtesy of San Bernardino County Safety Employees Benefit Association.)

In 1919, the county board of supervisors authorized purchase of an automobile for the sheriff. A big Studebaker sedan was bought, but Sheriff Shay did not bother or want to learn to drive and thus used deputies for drivers. (Courtesy of Patrick Dailey.)

In 1919, the National Prohibition Act became the less than popular law of the land. Sheriff Walter Shay established a "dry squad AKA booze squad" that worked closely with federal, state, and local agencies to fight the scourge of alcoholic beverages. It has been said that it was not uncommon for a substantial portion of the confiscated booze to disappear before it made it to the evidence room. (Courtesy of San Bernardino County Safety Employees Benefit Association.)

Barstow deputy Prichart is depicted here c. 1923. (Courtesy of San Bernardino County Sheriff's Department.)

Needles deputy George Acuna was captured in this photograph around 1924. (Courtesy of San Bernardino County Safety Employees Benefit Association.)

The sheriff's office personnel poses for the camera around 1924. (Courtesy of San Bernardino County Safety Employees Benefit Association.)

The prohibition of the manufacture, sale, and transportation of alcoholic beverages occurred with the 18th Amendment, which was repealed in 1933. Here is a "Dry Squad" raid in the 1920s. (Courtesy of San Bernardino County Safety Employees Benefit Association.)

Occasionally known as the "Booze Squad," this group conducts a raid in the 1920s. (Courtesy of San Bernardino County Safety Employees Benefit Association.)

Deputy R. A. "Dick" Bright, pictured here in the 1920s, was known for having once "with nothing more than a shotgun, marched eighty men who'd commandeered a train at Yermo into jail in San Bernardino." (Courtesy of San Bernardino County Safety Employees Benefit Association.)

Deputies are depicted standing in front of sheriff's office and jail in the 1920s. (Courtesy of San Bernardino County Safety Employees Benefit Association.)

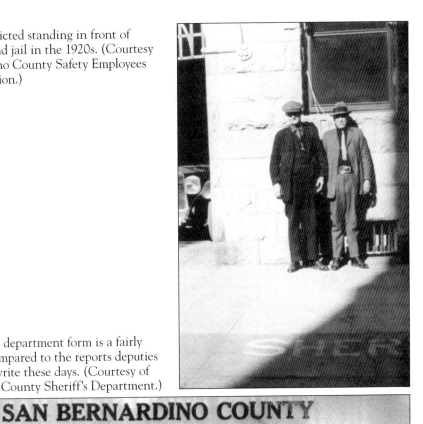

This prohibition department form is a fairly simple report compared to the reports deputies are required to write these days. (Courtesy of San Bernardino County Sheriff's Department.)

SAN BERNARDINO COUNTY
Prohibition Enforcement Dept.

Name ....

Address ....

City or Town ....

Date of Sale .... Time ....

Quantity .... Price ....

Money Used ....

Witnesses ....

Chemist ....

Alcohol ....

In the 1920s, Wyatt Earp frequented Vidal as he worked his nearby Happy Days Mine. On one occasion in the 1920s, local constable James Wilson came to see Wyatt, who was in his 70s, to ask for assistance in arresting a suspect who was in the process of robbing a nearby store. A hasty plan called for the constable to cover the rear door and apprehend the suspect as he fled when Wyatt entered the front door. The plan didn't quite work out. Wyatt entered the store and "ordered" the suspect to surrender his firearm. He complied, and Wyatt physically escorted him outside into Constable Wilson's custody. The constable received the appropriate amount of teasing, and word of the incident reached Sheriff Walter Shay, who "sent congratulations" and invited Wyatt to drop by his office at his convenience. Some weeks later, Wyatt visited the sheriff's office and found him to be out of town. The privilege of presenting a badge to Wyatt went to Undersheriff Tom Carter. (Courtesy of *True West.*)

San Bernardino County traffic officer/deputy sheriffs are depicted here around 1925. (Courtesy of Patrick Dailey.)

Sheriff Shay established the identification division in 1921 when he hired Deputy O. W. Bottoroff from Fresno County. Bottoroff was a highly respected forensic specialist, who served under all three Sheriff Shays until his retirement in 1945. (Courtesy of Patrick Dailey.)

Hired in 1915, several decades before affirmative action, Deputy Jesus Amarias was very loyal and served for more than 30 years under five sheriffs, including all three Shays. He was known to be very skilled at man tracking, and the press occasionally referred to him as the sheriff's "faithful Indian scout." He resented this title as he considered himself a Mexican American. For some years, Sheriff Walter Shay, who preferred revolvers, was annoyed that Amarias persisted in carrying a German Luger pistol that he had received from a World War I veteran. Amarias was also known for just carrying a Winchester .30-30 lever-action rifle along with a fabric bag loaded with cartridges. (Courtesy of Patrick Dailey.)

SOUVENIR PROGRAM

OFFICIAL OPENING

OF THE

SAN BERNARDINO COUNTY COURT HOUSE

AND

UNVEILING OF THE MEMORIAL TABLET

DEDICATING THE SITE

· SATURDAY · APRIL 30th, 1927 ·

This is a program for the San Bernardino County Courthouse opening ceremony. (Courtesy of Patrick Dailey.)

San Bernardino County Courthouse construction began in 1926, and the facility opened for service in 1927. The county jail was located on the top floor of the new courthouse and is the sheriff's longest-serving jail at more than 79 years. It is used today as an auxiliary jail for courthouse holding and in case of emergency. (Courtesy of San Bernardino County Museum.)

The San Bernardino County Courthouse is seen here some years later. (Courtesy of San Bernardino County Museum.)

Sheriff's office personnel pose for the camera in 1927. (Courtesy of San Bernardino County Safety Employees Benefit Association.)

San Bernardino County traffic officer/deputy sheriffs are pictured behind the courthouse in 1927. Their names and patrol areas are, from left to right, George Carpenter (Ontario), Clint Kingman (Rialto), Frank J. Freeman (Cucamonga), Louis Kronemeyer (Upland), Jack Marks (Colton), Capt. Jay Boone (Redlands), Dale Pence (Redlands), Ralph Craig Milles (Ontario), James "Pat" Patterson (Highland), Harry Hanson (San Bernardino), and Smiley Hancock (San Bernardino). In 1929, most of these traffic officer/deputy sheriffs were absorbed into the newly organized California Highway Patrol. (Courtesy of Richard Bise.)

Sheriff Ernest T. Shay, who served as the top lawman from 1931 to 1934, was the nephew of Sheriff Walter Shay. He reluctantly assumed the position of sheriff after the county board of supervisors appointed him to serve out the remainder of his uncle's term. (Courtesy of Patrick Dailey.)

Sheriff Ernest Shay is pictured at a Western function. (Courtesy of San Bernardino County Safety Employees Benefit Association.)

The Baldy Mesa shoot-out of April 27, 1934, came about after two inmates escaped from San Quentin Prison, kidnapped two San Rafael policemen, and headed south. The two policemen were dropped off in San Bernardino, and then the fugitives robbed a drugstore. They were "heavily armed" and stated they would not go back to prison. They drove north over Cajon Pass and were intercepted by the Victorville sheriff's posse riding in a 1932 Ford V-8. The posse pursued the suspects in the Desoto coupe towards Victorville on old Highway 66. A running gun battle ensued, and the escapees made good on their vow not to return to prison. Note the bullet holes, missing tires, and blood and gore on the vehicle's windows. (Courtesy of Patrick Dailey.)

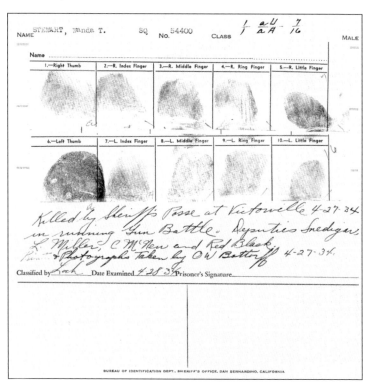

NAME STEWART, Wanda T.   SQ   No. 54400   CLASS 1 a 4 7 / 1 a A 16   MALE

Name ....

| 1.—Right Thumb | 2.—R. Index Finger | 3.—R. Middle Finger | 4.—R. Ring Finger | 5.—R. Little Finger |
| 6.—Left Thumb | 7.—L. Index Finger | 8.—L. Middle Finger | 9.—L. Ring Finger | 10.—L. Little Finger |

Killed by Sheriff's Posse at Victorville 4-27-34 in running Gun Battle. Deputies Snedigar, L. Miller, C. McNew and Red Black. Prints + Photographs taken by O.W. Bettorff 4-27-34.

Classified by .... Date Examined 4-28-34 Prisoner's Signature ....

BUREAU OF IDENTIFICATION DEPT., SHERIFF'S OFFICE, SAN BERNARDINO, CALIFORNIA

This is the fingerprint card of one of the deceased escapees. Note the wording of "sheriff's posse" on the card, still being used in the 1930s. (Courtesy of Patrick Dailey.)

The Baldy Mesa posse members pictured here, from left to right, are Deputy Stan Snedigar and special deputies Lou Miller, Red Black, and Carl McNew. (Courtesy of San Bernardino County Sheriff's Department.)

Sheriff Emmett Shay served the county from 1934 to 1946. He would be the last of the Shays to hold the office of sheriff. A significant portion of the sheriff's office duties during the World War II years would be dealing with home front security and the increasing population that came with industrialization for the war effort. (Courtesy of Patrick Dailey.)

Sheriff Emmett Shay examines a revolver in his office. (Courtesy of Patrick Dailey.)

The Sheriff's Rangers were established by Emmett Shay in 1934. It is believed the posse came about as a result of Los Angeles County sheriff Eugene Biscaluiz's founding of his Mounted Silver Posse in 1933. The Sheriff's Rangers are the original reserves and the longest-serving reserve unit. (Courtesy of Patrick Dailey.)

Dismounted Sheriff's Rangers pose for the camera. Future sheriff James W. Stocker is wearing the dark hat. (Courtesy of Patrick Dailey.)

Sheriff Emmett Shay takes receipt of a 1937 Ford "woody," as well as Lincolns and Mercurys. (Courtesy of San Bernardino County Sheriff's Department.)

Members of the San Bernardino County Sheriff's Office take receipt of several 1937 Fords behind the county courthouse. (Courtesy of San Bernardino County Sheriff's Department.)

The old Victorville Sheriff's Office was originally a homestead shack that Constable Edward Dolch had moved to his property on Seventh Street. For over four decades, it was used as a residence for several families. The county leased the small structure in 1939, maintaining offices for several agencies at the same time. (Courtesy of Arthur Banks.)

Sheriff Emmett Shay and Los Angeles County sheriff Eugene Biscaluiz pose with a few ladies at a sheriff's social function. (Courtesy of Patrick Dailey.)

The mounted sheriffs pictured here, from left to right, are Riverside County sheriff Carl Rayburn, Los Angeles County sheriff Eugene Biscaluiz, and San Bernardino County sheriff Emmett Shay. (Courtesy of San Bernardino County Sheriff's Department.)

This is Sheriff Emmett Shay (second from the right) with executives, politicians, and a California Highway Patrol official at the Kaiser Steel mills in Fontana around 1942. (Courtesy of Patrick Dailey.)

Sheriff Emmett Shay inspects a train wreck near Cajon Pass. (Courtesy of Patrick Dailey.)

Sheriff Emmett Shay is depicted here in a Western-style portrait. (Courtesy of Suzanna Juarez.)

Local constables or deputy sheriffs are pictured here, c. 1943, standing on the porch of the Victorville sheriff's office. At right, a U.S. government military police station has replaced the previous brick building. (Courtesy of Patrick Dailey.)

West End deputies pose in the newly adopted San Bernardino County sheriff's uniform. This was the first standardized uniform for the sheriff's office. (Courtesy of Patrick Dailey.)

Sheriff Emmett Shay is pictured wearing the new sheriff's uniform. (Courtesy of Patrick Dailey.)

The Sheriff's Rangers strike up a pose with their mounts behind the San Bernardino County

The Sheriff's Rangers enjoy a chuck wagon function with Newt Bass, a wealthy land developer. (Courtesy of Patrick Dailey.)

Courthouse. (Courtesy of Patrick Dailey.)

Among the men at this Sheriff's Rangers formal dinner function are Sheriff Emmett Shay and

Newt Bass. (Courtesy of Patrick Dailey.)

Sheriff Emmett Shay waves goodbye as he rides into the sunset of his career. (Courtesy of Patrick Dailey.)

Three

THE TRANSITIONAL YEARS
1947–1955

Sheriffs James Stocker and Eugene Mueller represent the transitional period of the sheriff's office. Both brought different experiences and personalities to the job. Pictured is Sheriff Stocker's presentation diamond badge, which was one of many special badges worn by various sheriffs over the years.

Sheriff James W. Stocker, 1946–1950, took office during the initial years of the cold war and civil defense became the buzzword around the nation. With the passing of the Civil Defense Act, Sheriff Stocker activated additional reserve and auxiliary units within the sheriff's office. (Courtesy of Patrick Dailey.)

Deputy Carl McNew was a throwback to the Old West style of lawman. "He wore a Colt .44 on his hip with two concealed weapons under his shirt," one account explained. McNew dealt deliberately with criminals and was short with words. He was involved in the Baldy Mesa shoot-out of 1934 as well as several other gunfights and shootings. His reputation preceded him, so that when he entered a public place the room would go silent in anticipation or fear of someone being shot. (Courtesy of Patrick Dailey.)

Newt Bass's arrival at the Apple Valley Airport was met by an escort—members of the Apple Valley sheriff's posse. Bass is seated in the buggy at left with Los Angeles County sheriff Eugene Biscaluiz seated at right. (Courtesy of Mojave River Valley Museum.)

Sheriff Stocker and his wife, Vera, are dressed up to attend a Western-themed function. (Courtesy of Suzanna Juarez.)

Sheriff Stocker is depicted here with the jail cook, Bert "Curly" Crandall. Curly was known for being quite a character and for serving up good chow. (Courtesy of Suzanna Juarez.)

The garish attire on Sheriff Stocker had to do with his participation in a local event called "Covered Wagon Days." (Courtesy of Suzanna Juarez.)

Sheriff Stocker strikes up a gunfighter pose. (Courtesy of Suzanna Juarez.)

Sheriff Stocker, seen at right next to the jail chef, was photographed here in 1949 with all his deputies, who were brought together for this photograph. Arrangements were made with other agencies to handle calls for service during the shoot. The sheriff's office had 55 full-time deputies. (Courtesy of Paul Wilson.)

Deputy C. B. Juarez and another deputy fingerprint American Legionnaires who are signing on to be reserves for Sheriff Stocker. (Courtesy of Suzanna Juarez.)

Deputy C. B. Juarez's career was in the identification bureau. Here he is in 1950, photographing a subject for a mug shot. (Courtesy of Suzanna Juarez.)

Deputy Charles E. "Charley" Jones, depicted here c. 1950, was one of those notorious deputies who causes "headaches" for supervisors. He was well known for his mischief and pranks, some of the acts printable and others not. Most of the stories involve his duty performance under both Sheriffs Mueller and Bland. One stunt included shooting holes into his campaign hat after the wind blew it off and then planting a geranium in it after receiving desk duty as punishment. Sheriff Mueller wasn't amused and promptly assigned Charley to Amboy as the resident deputy. Amboy, as locals understand, is located in the Mojave, midway between Barstow and Needles. While in Amboy, Charley managed to accumulate discarded vehicle tires, which he deposited in the Amboy crater. He fired them up, causing quite a stir as folks far and near thought there was an active volcano in San Bernardino County. He was also known for standing alongside Highway 40 and rendering a most proper salute as Sheriff Bland motored by en route to Needles. Despite his mischievousness, Charley retired honorably in 1966, having rendered 20 years of service. (Courtesy of Patrick Dailey.)

Deputy John N. Carnahan, seen here around 1949, was disabled with the amputation of his left arm. However, decades before the American Disabilities Act, Sheriff Stocker saw fit to employ him as a "jailor." He would go on to serve as a courtroom bailiff under Sheriff Mueller. (Courtesy of Patrick Dailey.)

Deputies Martin and John Carnahan perform jail administrative duties in 1949. (Courtesy of Patrick Dailey.)

These deputies appear to be discussing a criminal investigation, or at least posing as if they are involved in such a discussion, inside Substation 1 at Cucamonga in 1950. (Courtesy of Patrick Dailey.)

This photograph depicts deputies in a 1950 Ford patrol car. (Courtesy of San Bernardino County Sheriff's Department.)

Deputies Bert Smith and Paul Wilson arrested this suspect during a burglary in progress in early morning hours. The suspect in the white shirt and handcuffs was attempting to do a "safe job" at the White Barn Furniture Store in San Bernardino. Pictured, from left to right, are Deputies Robert White, Paul Wilson, Everette Wade, Bert Smith, and Frank Liston. (Courtesy of Paul Wilson.)

Losing his bid for reelection in 1950, Sheriff Stocker appears to be saying farewell as he prepares to return to the ranch. (Courtesy of Patrick Dailey.)

Sheriff Eugene Mueller had an impressive law-enforcement career. He had previously served as Upland's chief of police from 1941 until assuming office as San Bernardino County's sheriff in 1951. After losing his reelection to Frank Bland in 1954, he served with Culver City as chief of police from 1956 until his retirement in 1970. Sheriff Mueller brought changes to the sheriff's office—some were well received and others not. He was very cognizant of professional appearance, thorough investigations, and dedicated duty performance. He was a visionary of sorts as he contemplated the future of law enforcement and changes that would modernize the sheriff's office. (Courtesy of Patrick Dailey.)

On Monday, April 14, 1952, Sheriff Mueller conducted "the first full dress inspection in the history of the San Bernardino County Sheriff's Office," according to a report. Held on the front lawn of the courthouse, the inspection was "attended by city and county officials and visiting police officers." Officials included members of the board of supervisors and grand jury, as well as judges, the mayor, and the chief of police. (Courtesy of Paul Wilson.)

Sheriff Mueller is pictured inspecting deputies as Inspector H. C. "Bud" English follows behind. The deputies are holding "first of its kind" rules and regulations manuals for the sheriff's office. (Courtesy of Patrick Dailey.)

Sheriff Mueller is seen inspecting the female personnel whose duty assignments were as jail matrons and in clerical and records staff positions. (Courtesy of Suzanna Juarez.)

Here the sheriff's color guard wears both winter and summer uniforms. (Courtesy of Patrick Dailey.)

These deputies, from left to right, are Robert Woods, Lester Leiss, Wayne Matthewson, and Joseph Glines. The majority of the deputies did not care for the newly adopted wool campaign hats or tropical worsted tan uniforms. The uniforms looked terrible after perspiring on a summer day, and the wool campaign hat was annoying and uncomfortable on warm days. It was required wearing inside the patrol car and outdoors. After Sheriff Mueller left office, a bonfire was built behind the courthouse fueled by wool campaign hats. Thus very few specimens have survived. (Courtesy of Patrick Dailey.)

Sheriff Mueller poses in a 1952 Chevy patrol car at the Orange Show grounds in San Bernardino. (Courtesy of Patrick Dailey.)

The Sheriff's Aero-Squadron reserve unit was established on August 15, 1952, and still exists today within the aviation division. Sheriff Muller is pictured here pinning on the squadron's new wings at a formal function. (Courtesy of Patrick Dailey.)

Sheriff Mueller is pictured at the groundbreaking ceremony in 1952 for the Wrightwood Sheriff's Reserve headquarters building. (Courtesy of Patrick Dailey.)

The Wrightwood Sheriff's Substation in the early 1950s was a resident deputy assignment and remained so into the 1990s. (Courtesy of Patrick Dailey.)

Sheriff Mueller is seen with Chief Lester Leiss and dignitaries in desert. (Courtesy of Patrick Dailey.)

Sheriff Mueller addresses the Tri-County Posse in the desert. The posse was made up of both mounted and motorcycle members. (Courtesy of Patrick Dailey.)

The Women's Sheriff's Reserve, Fontana District, was organized in October 1953. (Courtesy of Patrick Dailey.)

This is Chief Lester Leiss with the Sheriff's Drum and Bugle Corps. There weren't enough musically talented deputies to pull this off, so the corps was composed of volunteers from the community. (Courtesy of San Bernardino County Safety Employees Benefit Association.)

Deputy Donald Myers and Capt. Cecil Myers strike a pose. Thus far, the Meyers family has provided three generations of deputy sheriffs. (Courtesy of Patrick Dailey.)

Deputies amuse themselves at the expense of this deceased black bear before it became jailhouse stew. It was standard practice to bring road-kill critters or otherwise dispatched game animals back to the jail or county hospital to feed the inmates or patients. (Courtesy of Suzanna Juarez.)

The first regular transportation detail was established in 1952 with this vehicle, a 1952 Chevrolet station wagon. Today the transportation division has a fleet of buses, vans, and sedans to transport inmates throughout the state. (Courtesy of Patrick Dailey.)

Sheriff Mueller, being somewhat eccentric or flamboyant, is pictured here alongside Chief Lester Leiss wearing a pith helmet. He was also known for using a starting pistol or whistle on occasion and for shouting "Geronimo" over the radio as the code word to initiate a raid on a gambling establishment. Mueller is credited with cleaning up most of the longtime gambling and prostitution establishments. (Courtesy of Patrick Dailey.)

Looking down onto the county courthouse lawn is Sheriff Mueller and an entourage with the color guard and drum and bugle corps. This conspicuous display caused quite a stir in the courthouse as the corps entered with resounding brass and drums. (Courtesy of Duane Mellinger.)

Another shot depicts the sheriff and his entourage with the color guard and drum and bugle corps. This ceremony came about as a result of Sheriff Mueller being informed that one of his deputies was going to be awarded the Bronze Star for heroism during the Korean War. (Courtesy of Duane Mellinger.)

Maj. Gen. E. C. Langmead, commander of Norton Air Force Base, presents the Bronze Star to Deputy Duane Mellinger. (Courtesy of Duane Mellinger.)

Inspector H. C. English, Deputy Duane Mellinger, and Sheriff Mueller are pictured here after the presentation of the Bronze Star. (Courtesy of Duane Mellinger.)

Sheriff Eugene Mueller and future undersheriff Kendall Stone are pictured at a Sheriff's Rangers function in the Big Bear Valley. (Courtesy of Patrick Dailey.)

Sheriff Eugene Mueller pins the badge on newly elected Sheriff Frank Bland. (Courtesy of San Bernardino County Sheriff's Department.)

Four

THE FRANK BLAND ERA
1955–1983

Sheriff Frank Bland was often compared to western movie icon John Wayne. However, unlike the "Duke," Bland did not just talk it, he walked it. He seemed larger than life, and his career as a peace officer is legendary throughout the county. He was elected sheriff seven times—a total of 28 years. Pictured is his presentation diamond badge. (Courtesy of San Bernardino County Sheriff's Department.)

Sheriff Frank Bland served San Bernardino County from 1955 to 1983. He had previously served as a U.S. Marine Corps gunnery sergeant during World War II for three years in the Pacific Theatre. He saw action on Iwo Jima and Okinawa, which resulted in his being wounded three times. Prior to being discharged, he was notified that he was appointed chief of police of Needles. He also served as a special deputy before his run for sheriff. (Courtesy of Patrick Dailey.)

Sheriff Frank Bland and Deputy Willard Farquar enjoy some conversation at the Crestline Station in 1955. (Courtesy of Duane Mellenger.)

Reserve deputy Bill Newberry, Sgt. Robby Robinson, and reserve deputy George Boyner of the Apple Valley Sheriff's posse appear to be discussing the situation, c. 1956. (Courtesy of Patrick Dailey.)

Sheriff Frank Bland is seen here at the Orange Show for the first sheriff's rodeo in 1957. Bland introduced the rodeo, and it was held annually until 1971. (Courtesy of Patrick Dailey.)

The San Bernardino County Sheriff's training class of 1958 pose for this photograph. The training at the time lasted only a couple of weeks and was conducted at the courthouse. (Courtesy of Patrick Dailey.)

The Apple Valley Posse is seen here in 1960. (Courtesy of Patrick Dailey.)

Sheriff Frank Bland examines a knife as part of some contraband and dope seized by his deputies. At that time, this was considered to be a significant narcotics investigation, but it pales in comparison to the investigations of today. (Courtesy of Patrick Dailey.)

The sheriff's command-post truck is seen here along with reserve deputies who stand by to respond to emergencies. (Courtesy of Patrick Dailey.)

A deputy examines a map with his faithful search dog at his side. (Courtesy of Patrick Dailey.)

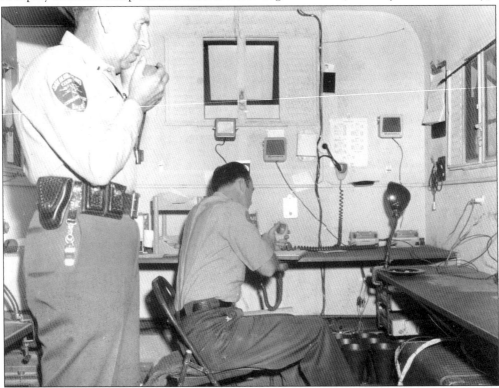

Both reserve and regular deputies work together in the command-post truck. (Courtesy of Patrick Dailey.)

Reserve deputy Billy Heckle became the first San Bernardino County deputy sheriff to die in the line of duty, on January 1, 1960. He was shot to death in a Bloomington citrus grove while covering another deputy. Since then, another nine deputies and two search-and-rescue volunteers have died in the line of duty. This photograph of Billy was obtained in 2005, 45 years after the incident. (Courtesy of Steven Jaronski.)

This is opening day at the Glen Helen Rehabilitation Center in 1960. Many of the officers pictured are former county road camp guards. They were merged into the sheriff's office as custody deputies. (Courtesy of Patrick Dailey.)

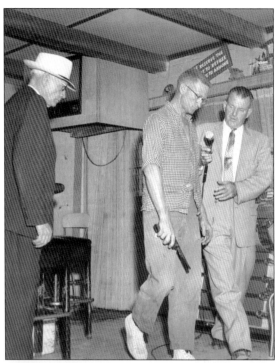

Sheriff Frank Bland is pictured here conducting a crime-scene reenactment, c. 1963. He was one of the pioneers of this investigative technique, which he had introduced to the Identification Bureau in 1959. Sheriff Bland was also one of the earliest to introduce color mug shots. (Courtesy of Patrick Dailey.)

Frank Bland inspects the trunk of a patrol car. Note the Winchester rifle in the trunk. This was the standard-issue rifle from the late 19th century into the early 1980s. (Courtesy of Patrick Dailey.)

This is the Morongo Sheriff's Station in the 1960s. Moved to a modern facility and renamed the Morongo Basin Station, today it provides police services for two contract cities and the unincorporated county areas of the Morongo valley and environs. (Courtesy of Patrick Dailey.)

The Needles Sheriff's Station, depicted here in the 1960s, would eventually be replaced by a modern facility and renamed the Colorado River Station. The station is responsible for servicing the Mojave Desert and the "East Coast." (Courtesy of Patrick Dailey.)

Deputies Jerome "Punch" Ringhofer and Chuck Woodman are depicted in 1963 at the Big Bear Station. The Thompson submachine gun was station issue. (Courtesy of Patrick Dailey.)

The San Bernardino County Sheriff's Chris-Craft motorboats are pictured operating on Lake Arrowhead in 1964. (Courtesy of Patrick Dailey.)

The sheriff's scuba divers were sometimes referred to as the "underwater squad." Pictured here in 1964, they conduct training at Lake Arrowhead. (Courtesy of Patrick Dailey.)

Reserve deputies are standing by for deployment to roadblocks during forest fires. (Courtesy of Patrick Dailey.)

Sheriff's deputies practice at the range, shooting weapons during their monthly qualification course. Shooting techniques have dramatically improved since then. (Courtesy of Patrick Dailey.)

Sheriff Frank Bland poses with the staff at the station of the first contract city of Victorville in 1965. (Courtesy of Patrick Dailey.)

Around 1965, an Anti-Sniper Squad (ASS) was formed as a result of the civil unrest of the 1960s, utilizing jeeps with .50-caliber machine guns. For obvious reasons, several months later, the name was changed to Special Enforcement Detail (SED). The detail is pictured above in 1965. (Courtesy of Patrick Dailey.)

For many years prior to the establishment of a training academy, Glen Helen Rehabilitation Center served as the location for the basic academy. (Courtesy of Patrick Dailey.)

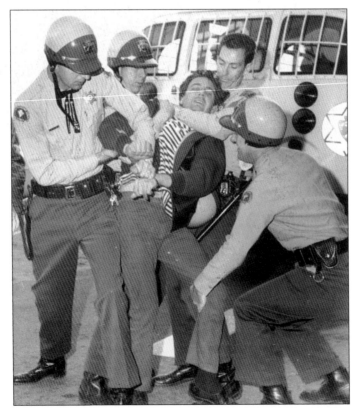

Deputies are pictured subduing a difficult subject. Although it appears staged, a *Sun-Telegram* reporter, who happened to be on this February 18, 1967, scene, took the photograph. (Courtesy of Patrick Dailey.)

Inspector Paul Wilson examines an AK-47 assault rifle with a firearms specialist at the FBI Academy in 1971. Numerous department management personnel have attended the academy over the years. (Courtesy of Paul Wilson.)

Deputy Pat Dailey is on patrol near Wrightwood in the winter of 1977. The vast expanses of the county required deputies to be equipped and ready to work in any area and in all weather conditions. (Courtesy of Patrick Dailey.)

The West End Search and Rescue Team, pictured here, was originally composed of regular deputy sheriffs before transitioning to reserve unit status. Today there are several types of search-and-rescue (S&R) units. They are composed of reserve deputies and sheriff's volunteers for response to any type of emergency situation. These units include aviation, cave, desert, mountain, urban, mounted posse, scuba, and K-9 search-and-rescue capabilities.

In Memory of
Deputy James B. Evans
and the
Heroes of the
May 9, 1980
Norco Bank Robbery

A True Hero

May 9, 1980, is a day that will long be remembered in Norco and throughout the law enforcement community nation-wide. The bank robbery that took place here drew police officers and deputies from across the Inland Empire into a running gun-battle that is still one of the most violent in American history. There were many heroes that day, including Deputy Jim Evans, who pursued the gunmen with perseverance. Deputy Evans lost his life in the final confrontation, but the memory of his heroism will live on forever.

Remembering May 9, 1980
The Norco Bank Robbery

Officers Wounded

Glyn Bolasky, rso   Herman Brown, rso
Rolf Parkes, rso   Ken McDaniels, rso
Tony Reynard, rso   D.J. McCarty, sbso
Darrel Reed, rso   Bill Crowe, chp

And for the many other law enforcement personnel who risked their lives that day

Depending on which side of the county line one is on, this running gunfight is known as the Norco bank robbery or Lytle Creek shoot-out. It started with gunfire being exchanged in Norco on May 9, 1980, followed by a lengthy pursuit, and more gunfights that ended at Lytle Creek the following day. Five suspects were involved; two were slain and three arrested. More than 30 patrol units and one aircraft were damaged or destroyed during the pursuit. Riverside County deputy James B. Evans was killed in a hasty ambush at the end of the vehicle pursuit. Many lessons were learned from this incident and changes came about in interagency communications and tactics. Winchester Mod. 94 rifles were traded in for Ruger Mini-14 rifles, and Immediate Response Teams (IRTs) were organized. (Courtesy of author.)

The department's first Exceptional Service Awards ceremony was held at Redlands University on October 21, 1981. The first Frank Bland Medal of Valor recipients were six deputies who are identified by the ribbons with medals attached. Pictured, from left to right, are Deputies Ron Hazard, Ken Schreckengost, Dan McCarty, Ron Belter, Mike Cordua, and William Meals. The Frank Bland Medal of Valor was developed by the Sheriff's Employees Benefit Association, the awarding authority for the medal. (Courtesy of Ken Schreckengost.)

Sheriff Frank Bland is seen at home on the range. (Courtesy of San Bernardino County Sheriff's Department.)

Five

"DEDICATED
TO YOUR SAFETY"
1983–2000

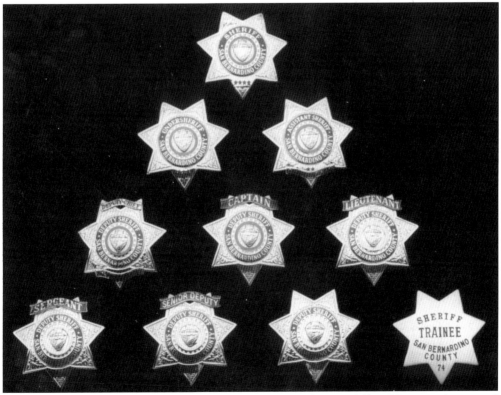

The sheriffs that served after Sheriff Frank Bland had a tough act to follow. However, they served with distinction during the last years of the 20th century. Sheriff Floyd Tidwell served the first eight years, followed by Sheriff Richard "Dick" Williams for four years, and Sheriff Gary Penrod for the last five. Each brought their own personality and style to the department. Pictured are the badge styles adopted by Sheriff Tidwell after taking office in 1983. (Courtesy of San Bernardino County Sheriff's Department.)

Sheriff Floyd Tidwell, 1983 to 1990, had served in the department for more than 30 years when he was elected sheriff. He brought several changes to the department including the motto, "Dedicated to Your Safety," and officially changed the title of sheriff's office to sheriff's department. He created a new unit called the Career Criminal Division and introduced new blue-striped patrol cars (units), which were sometimes referred to as "gas company or plain wrap" units due to the similarity in color scheme. He was fond of the color blue and a directive was put out that only he could use blue ink, which became his signature trademark. As cities contracted for sheriff's services, they liked having their own color scheme on the patrol units, and a fleet of "circus wagons" was seen about the county. (Courtesy of Patrick Dailey.)

The Special Weapons and Tactics (SWAT) team, pictured here at the special operations training facility, was located at the sheriff's range. The facility consisted of a tower and a tire house for live-fire exercises as well as several ranges. The SWAT concept was adopted by the sheriff's department, and initially the team came from the Central Patrol Station in San Bernardino. Sheriff Tidwell formed a new unit identified as the Career Criminal Division (CCD), which assumed the SWAT mission. Years later, CCD reorganized with the narcotics division and retained the SWAT role. (Courtesy of James Stalnaker.)

The Special Operations Training Facility's tower is being used by SWAT personnel for a rappelling exercise. (Courtesy of William Kidd.)

SWAT team members conduct a helicopter-insertion exercise with the aviation division. (Courtesy of William Kidd.)

SWAT team members pose in front of the San Bernardino Hell's Angels clubhouse after successfully conducting a high-risk warrant service. (Courtesy of Jim Collins.)

Deputy Steven Cobine of Humboldt County and the author are depicted during a tactical field exercise in the San Bernardino Mountains. In 1985, the sheriff's department training division hosted the California Department of Justice's courses called Campaign Against Marijuana Planting (CAMP). A specialized cadre, as well as instructors, was selected from both the department and outside personnel. The student raid team leaders were drawn from outside agencies that would be conducting operations throughout the state, including in North California's "Emerald Triangle"—Humboldt, Mendocino, and Trinity Counties—the largest marijuana-growing area in the United States. As the growing of marijuana became more profitable, Marijuana Eradication Teams (MET) were formed to address the problem during the growing season in the local mountains. (Courtesy of author.)

Deputy Richard Buzzard of the Victorville Station is seen here with an Attack Drunk Driving (ADD) unit. ADD was organized as a multiagency task force that specialized in targeting drunk drivers. It was shown to be very effective, and ADD task forces are still deployed today. (Courtesy of San Bernardino County Sheriff's Department.)

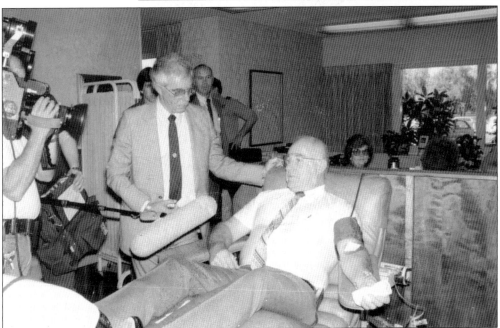

Sheriff Tidwell, seen here donating blood while being interviewed by the news media, implemented a department blood-donor program that continues today. (Courtesy of San Bernardino County Sheriff's Department.)

Sheriff Tidwell and the San Bernardino police chief Don Burnett square off before the annual "Pig Bowl" football game. The event was conducted for a number of years with the police and other agencies as a fund-raiser. (Courtesy of San Bernardino County Sheriff's Department.)

Lt. James Stalnaker meets with then Vice President George Bush during the future president's visit to San Bernardino County. Lieutenant Stalnaker was responsible for the SWAT team's dignitary-protection liaison with the U.S. Secret Service. (Courtesy of James Stalnaker.)

The sheriff's headquarters building opened in 1987 and serves as the home for administration and records divisions, several specialized investigative divisions, and the central patrol division. (Courtesy of San Bernardino County Sheriff's Department.)

This 1988 photograph is from opening day for the contract Hesperia Station. (Courtesy of Patrick Dailey.)

Among many new training programs introduced to department personnel was the cross-cultural communications course. The course was five days in duration and attended by several agencies' sworn personnel. It was designed to better relationships between the expanding Hispanic community and law-enforcement agencies. (Courtesy of author.)

Sheriff Floyd Tidwell is seen here on parade. (Courtesy of Patrick Dailey.)

Sheriff Tidwell is tall in the saddle for this public-relations photograph. (Courtesy of San Bernardino County Sheriff's Department.)

Sheriff Richard "Dick" Williams, who served the county from 1990 to 1994, had been in the department for 25 years prior to assuming the top post. He brought sound ideas to the department but alienated some folks during the process. A new logo consisting of a sheriff's star in motion, with black and gold trimmings, was adopted and is still used today. It was rumored Sheriff Williams was attempting to form a "kinder, gentler, and more police-like" department, with western attire not being encouraged. A press release announcing a new "etiquette guide" for department personnel was met with hostility, humiliation, and humor. Sheriff Williams served only one term. (Courtesy of Patrick Dailey.)

Opening-day ceremonies are seen here in 1991 at the West Valley Detention Center in Rancho Cucamonga. With the central jail having served for 20 years, the new detention center became the primary custody facility in the county. It has a daily inmate population of 3,000 and is extensively staffed by deputies, custody specialists, nurses, and culinary and maintenance personnel. The Detention and Corrections Bureau is capable of housing over 5,000 inmates between its four facilities and is considered one of the "mega-jail" systems in the United States. (Courtesy of San Bernardino County Sheriff's Department.)

An aerial view clearly shows the octagonal-shaped modules that house the inmates. (Courtesy of San Bernardino County Sheriff's Department.)

An aerial view depicts the Emergency Vehicles Operations Center (EVOC). The facility opened in 1991 and is one of the largest emergency-vehicle training centers in the world. It was funded at no cost to the taxpayers and utilizes classrooms, state-of-the-art simulators, and an extensive series of roads and tracks for various training exercises. Numerous outside agencies have trained their officers here as well as civilian and commercial drivers. (Courtesy of San Bernardino County Sheriff's Department.)

This is the Sheriff's Region I Mobile Field Force (MFF) staged in the Central Detention Center's back lot on April 30, 1992, in preparation for deployment to the riots in Los Angeles. Pictured are the Adam-130 and Adam-131 teams of 1st Squad, 1st Platoon. Pictured, from left to right, are (first row) Sgt. Vic Holley and Cpl. John Navarro; (second row) Deputies Steve Geist, Carlos Espinoza, Robert Paprocki, the author, Rod Ivy, and Jon Carver. They deployed to the city of Inglewood, located in the south-central Los Angeles area. (Courtesy of author.)

Lt. Joe Henry of the San Bernardino County Sheriff's Department meets Pres. Bill Clinton as Lt. Ross Dvorak looks on. The president and other dignitaries often visit San Bernardino County, and the sheriff's protective detail coordinates with the U.S. Secret Service and other federal agencies to shield them from any prospective danger. (Courtesy of San Bernardino County Sheriff's Department.)

Sheriff Gary Penrod has served in San Bernardino County's top law-enforcement position since 1994. (Courtesy of San Bernardino County Sheriff's Department.)

Posing here are narcotics division deputies with a large haul of confiscated cocaine and marijuana. (Courtesy of San Bernardino County Sheriff's Department.)

Deputy Tony Acosta is seen here with his K-9 partner, Rocky. Privately owned working dogs were first deployed in search-and-rescue operations. In the 1980s, patrol dogs were introduced, but today the K-9s are primarily used for bomb and narcotics detection. (Courtesy of San Bernardino County Sheriff's Department.)

The Sheriff's Honor Guard poses outside the Sturges Auditorium in San Bernardino. (Courtesy of San Bernardino County Sheriff's Department.)

With the enforcement of the California Vehicle Code in an increasing number of contract cities, motor officers were needed and were established to meet the city's traffic-enforcement needs. (Courtesy of San Bernardino County Sheriff's Department.)

The sheriff's department has an ongoing custody contract with the U.S. Marshal's Service and transports their inmates to "Con Air." (Courtesy of San Bernardino County Sheriff's Department.)

Sheriff Penrod is seen here with Roy Rogers, the "King of the Cowboys." Local Victorville and Apple Valley regular, Rogers had been commissioned years earlier by Sheriff Frank Bland as an honorary deputy and sheriff. Floyd Tidwell made Roy a member of the Sheriff's Council, on which he continued to serve until his death on July 6, 1998. (Courtesy of San Bernardino County Sheriff's Department.)

Retired deputy chief Keith Bushey served as the last San Bernardino County marshal. In October 1999, as a result of state legislation, the marshal's personnel merged into the sheriff's department. Deputy chief Bushey had previously retired as both a commander from the Los Angeles Police Department and a colonel from the U.S. Marine Corps Reserve. (Courtesy of San Bernardino County Sheriff's Department.)

Six

MILLENNIUM AND BEYOND
2000–2006

With predictions of a worldwide computer meltdown, there was much apprehension as the millennium approached. Interagency preparations and training were conducted to address the potential disaster. Most people were relieved as the clock hit 12:00:01 a.m. and life continued on as normal. Sheriff Gary Penrod rode into the 21st century in style, hosting the 2000 Police and Fire Games, resurrecting the Sheriff's Rodeo, and continuing to meet the challenges of the new century. Seen here is the 2003 sesquicentennial badge. (Courtesy of San Bernardino County Sheriff's Department.)

Morgan Hawkins, Sheriff's Rodeo Queen 2000, makes a grand entrance as she disembarks from 40-King with the assistance of Deputy B. J. Meelker. Sheriff Penrod reintroduced the sheriff's rodeo, and it is going into its seventh year as of this writing. (Courtesy of San Bernardino County Sheriff's Department.)

As a result of the 9-11 terrorist attacks, a call went out for additional volunteer peace officers to bolster the ranks of the public-safety forces during the approaching 2002 XIX Olympic Winter Games in Salt Lake City, Utah. Sheriff Penrod met the challenge and assigned Lt. Paul Curry to put a contingent together. Deputies were asked to volunteer and serve as unsalaried Olympic police officers with the Utah Olympic Public Safety Command. Twenty-seven deputies volunteered to serve for the duration of the games. Concurrently commissioned as Utah peace officers, they were assigned to various venues during the games. Pictured here is the author at center, taking a photograph break with deputy U.S. marshals. They had just cleared the roof of a suspicious subject on a high-rise building. (Courtesy of author.)

Reserve deputy Sheriff William K. Newberry was the longest-serving member in the history of the San Bernardino County Sheriff's Department, putting in more than 56 years from 1946 to 2002. Newberry served under Sheriffs James Stocker, Eugene Mueller, Frank Bland, Floyd Tidwell, Richard Williams, and Gary Penrod. He held the rank of reserve deputy chief and was appointed as a special assistant to the sheriff. He also received numerous awards for his service, including two Distinguished Service Awards and the Frank Bland Meritorious Service Medal, as well as the Arrowhead Award. He was still serving when he died on August 6, 2002. (Courtesy of San Bernardino County Sheriff's Department.)

The Aviation Division H-3 helicopter provides a heavy-lift capability for emergency operations such as firefighting, search-and-rescue, or SWAT call outs. (Courtesy of San Bernardino County Sheriff's Department.)

On July 23, 2004, the Native Sons of the Golden West dedicated the original county jail cell at the San Bernardino Pioneer and Historical Society. The sheriff's department representatives, at left in civilian and period attire respectively, are Sgt. Richard "Dick" Bise (retired) and the author. (Courtesy of Steven Shaw.)

A forensic specialist processes a crime scene's materials at the sheriff's headquarters building. A suspect had conducted a drive-by shooting, firing numerous rounds into the building. He was arrested and prosecuted. (Courtesy of San Bernardino County Sheriff's Department.)

Deputy chief Sheree Stewart was the first female captain in the San Bernardino County Sheriff's Department and became the first female deputy chief in 2005. (Courtesy of San Bernardino County Sheriff's Department.)

Tall in the saddle, Sheriff Gary Penrod rides on the ranch. (Courtesy of San Bernardino County Sheriff's Department.)

A parting shot shows the author in 2006, conducting a department history presentation at the San Bernardino Pioneer and Historical Society. The author served as a deputy sheriff for 25 years and received his B.A. in History from California State University, Fullerton in 1977. He is an active member of the California Law Enforcement Historical Society, the National Outlaw Lawman Association, the Single Action Shooting Society, the Benevolent Order of Law Dawgs, and the San Berdoo Law Dawgs. He is also a retired U.S. Army Reserve captain and Vietnam combat veteran. (Courtesy of Richard Molony.)

BIBLIOGRAPHY

Adams, Ramon F. *Six-Guns and Saddle Leather*. Mineola, NY: Dover Publications, Inc., 1998.

Argus newspapers

Banks, L. A. *Policing the Old Mojave Desert*. Apple Valley, CA: Phoenix Printing, 1994.

Beattie, George W. and Helen Pruitt. *Heritage of the Valley: San Bernardino's First Century*. Oakland, CA: Biobooks, 1951.

Bell, Bob Boze. *The Illustrated Life and Times of Wyatt Earp*. Phoenix, AZ: Tri Star-Boze Publications Inc., 2000.

Bureau of Detention and Corrections 2003 Annual. San Bernardino, CA: SBCSD, 2003.

Century of Progress 1853–1953: San Bernardino County Sheriff's Office. San Bernardino, CA: SEBA, 1953.

Chaput, Don. *Virgil Earp: Western Peace Officer*. Encampment, WY: Affiliated Writers of America, Inc., 1994.

Crongeyer, Sven. *Six Gun Sound: The Early History of the Los Angeles County Sheriff's Department*. Fresno, CA: Craven Street Books, Linden Publishing, Inc., 2006.

Dyke, Dix Van. *Daggett: Life in a Mojave Frontier Town*. Baltimore, MD: The John Hopkins University Press, 1997.

Guardian newspapers

Ingersoll, Luther A. *Century Annals of San Bernardino County*. Los Angeles, 1904.

Kyle, Douglas E. *Historic Spots in California*. Stanford, CA: Stanford University Press, 1990.

Lawton, Harry. *Willie Boy: A Desert Manhunt*. Balboa Island, CA: Paisano Press, 1960.

Lyman, Edward Leo. *San Bernardino: The Rise and Fall of a California Community*. Signature Books, Inc., 1996.

Sandos, James A. and Larry E. Burgess. *The Hunt For Willie Boy: Indian-Hating and Popular Culture*. Norman, OK: University of Oklahoma Press, 1994.

San Bernardino Sheriff's Office 1853–1973. San Bernardino, CA: SEBA, 1973.

San Bernardino County Sheriff's Department 1990. San Bernardino, CA: SBCSD, 1990.

San Bernardino County Sheriff's Department 2000. San Bernardino, CA: SBCSD, 2000.

San Bernardino County Sheriff's Rodeo Programs. San Bernardino, CA: SBSO and SEBA, 1957–1971.

Sun newspapers

Silva, Lee A. *Wyatt Earp: A Biography of the Legend*. Santa Ana, CA: Graphic Publishers, 2002.

Tefertiller, Casey. *Wyatt Earp: The Life Behind the Legend*. New York, NY: John Wiley & Sons, Inc., 1997.

Thompson, Richard D. and Kathryn L. *Pioneer of the Mojave*. Apple Valley, CA: Desert Knolls Press, 1995.

Virgines, George E. *Badges of Law and Order*. Rapid City, SD: Cochran Publishing Company, 1987.

Walker, Clifford James. *One Eye Closed the Other Red: The California Bootlegging Years*. Barstow, CA: Back Door Publishing, 1999.

ACROSS AMERICA, PEOPLE ARE DISCOVERING SOMETHING WONDERFUL. *THEIR HERITAGE.*

Arcadia Publishing is the leading local history publisher in the United States. With more than 3,000 titles in print and hundreds of new titles released every year, Arcadia has extensive specialized experience chronicling the history of communities and celebrating America's hidden stories, bringing to life the people, places, and events from the past. To discover the history of other communities across the nation, please visit:

www.arcadiapublishing.com

Customized search tools allow you to find regional history books about the town where you grew up, the cities where your friends and family live, the town where your parents met, or even that retirement spot you've been dreaming about.